The Last
Love Poem
I Will Ever
Write

ALSO BY GREGORY ORR

Poetry

River Inside the River
Burning the Empty Nests
Gathering the Bones Together
The Red House
We Must Make a Kingdom of It
New and Selected Poems
City of Salt
Orpheus & Eurydice
The Caged Owl: New and Selected Poems
Concerning the Book That Is the Body of the Beloved
How Beautiful the Beloved

Prose

A Primer for Poets and Readers of Poetry
Poetry as Survival
The Blessing: A Memoir
Stanley Kunitz: An Introduction to the Poetry
Richer Entanglements: Essays and Notes on Poetry and Poems

The Last
Love Poem
I Will Ever
Write

P O E M S

Gregory Orr

W. W. NORTON & COMPANY

Independent Publishers Since 1923

New York | London

For information about permission to reproduce selections from this book, write to
Permissions, W. W. Norton & Company, Inc., 500 Fifth Avenue, New York, NY 10110

For information about special discounts for bulk purchases, please contact
W. W. Norton Special Sales at specialsales@wwnorton.com or 800-233-4830

Manufacturing by Lake Book Manufacturing
Book design by JAM Design
Production manager: Lauren Abbate

Library of Congress Cataloging-in-Publication Data

Names: Orr, Gregory, author.
Title: The last love poem I will ever write : poems / Gregory Orr.
Description: New York : W. W. Norton & Company, [2019]
Identifiers: LCCN 2018059611 | ISBN 9781324002352 (hardcover)
Classification: LCC PS3565.R7 A6 2019 | DDC 811/.54—dc23
LC record available at https://lccn.loc.gov/2018059611

W. W. Norton & Company, Inc., 500 Fifth Avenue, New York, N.Y. 10110
www.wwnorton.com

W. W. Norton & Company Ltd., 15 Carlisle Street, London W1D 3BS

1 2 3 4 5 6 7 8 9 0

FOR TRISHA

Contents

The Last
Love Poem
I Will Ever
Write

And So

"He's already in heaven," she said,
"Sitting down to feast with Jesus."
Back then, if I had been eight or ten
And she had been a peer instead
Of an adult, I might have said:
"You must have a hole in your head,"
Meaning: You must be crazy.

But I was twelve and though
I thought she was insane I was too
Polite and frightened to say as much.
And the hole was not a metaphor
But one a bullet had made that day
In my brother's head. And I
Was the one who put it there.

I wonder if she was thinking
Of the painted window
In our dinky church: the one
Where Jesus sat at a picnic table
With bread and a jug of something?
Was it an image of the Wedding
At Cana? Or the Last Supper
Before any of the other guests
Had arrived?
    He didn't look
Lonely, He just sat with His arms
Spread and His empty hands open

As if He was patiently waiting
For someone to put something in them:
A plate of food? Some nails? A gun?

Who knows what He was up to,
What He thought or felt?
He was in His world
And I was in mine.
This is all I knew that was true:
I was alive; my brother was dead.
When I closed my eyes I saw him
Lying at my feet.
                    I knew
God and I were through,
And after that, what is there?

I imagined I was floating
Alone in a vast abyss
Like a little cloud,
But I wasn't—I was falling
As fast as a material body can,
But the distance was infinite
And there was nothing near
By which to judge
What was happening, and so
It seemed I wasn't moving at all.

Song of What Happens

If I wrote in a short story
Or novel that when my father
Was young, about thirteen,
He and his best friend
Stole a rifle from the car trunk
Of a man who worked
For his family, then took
Paper plates from the kitchen
And went out to a field,
Intending to toss them
Into the air and shoot them . . .
That there'd been an accident
And he killed his best friend.

Sad, but believable—it happens
More often than you'd imagine
In the country.
                    But then I add:
My dad grew up, married,
Had four sons, gave each
Of the two oldest
Shotguns when they were
Twelve and ten
So they could all hunt pheasants.
And when I turned twelve,
He gave me a rifle—a .22.
And that same year
We went hunting deer

In a far field on our property
And my gun, that I didn't know
Was loaded, went off
And killed my younger brother
Who was standing beside me.
Two boys, my father and I,
Barely in their teens,
Killing two others they loved
By accident—that kind
Of coincidence isn't credible
In fiction, much less in a poem
Where you're not allowed
To describe too much
Or explain, or ascribe motives
Because each word is precious
And the fewer you use
The better the poem.
                    And yet,
I'm telling you it's true,
It really happened.
                    All of us
Can see the pattern here—
Two young boys kill
Someone they love
By accident.
                    But do you
Think God planned it?
And if so, why?
Do you think my father
Unconsciously arranged

A repetition, hoping
It would end differently?

I'm happy for you if you
Can explain it
To your satisfaction.
I can't.
    I'm only telling you
About it, because
It's factual; it happened.
And because I want you to know
How strange life is.

No use closing . . .

No use closing my eyes
Now—
    After
The lightning flash.

Wince and blinding—
They're both
Already inside me.

Dark Song

The heart, altering, alters all.

Sometimes, it happens and who
Knows why—the world
Suddenly turns ugly
And decides to crush you.

Don't waste time trying
To understand, just fight
For your life, do all you can
To survive.
          That's what
Jacob did on the riverbank
When he was ambushed
By that cruel angel.
            All night
He fought against a silent,
Giant malice that was
Determined to destroy him.

Yes, he came through it alive—
I'm with you on that:
By all means, let's celebrate
What a doughty human can do
Against impossible odds.

But who says the actual
Battle was the worst of it?
There's also aftermath.

I wish Jacob good luck
Trying to figure out
Why God would
Send such a creature to do
Such a job.
                    Maybe he got
A blessing; maybe not,
But I'm personally certain
Of this much:
                    As that
Bleak dawn came on
And he sat in the mud,
Recovering,
Rubbing his torn shoulder
And bruised legs,
Jacob's heart was filling
With a bitter
Wisdom
Blended of tears,
Rage, fear and shame.

For me, the only question is:

After that, what cup?
What cup could he drink from?

Song of Aftermath

Standing, now, in a place
Scrubbed raw by flood.

I, who sought neither
Rapture nor fracture.

Now the question is:
What to do with shatter?

Someone else's map?
I'd end up half-trapped;

And even the best often
Just guess what's next.

If I'm to grow now,
It will be through grieving;

It will be through this
Deepening I didn't choose.

Ode to Nothing

Sorrow makes children of us all—
the wisest knows nothing.
EMERSON

1. At the Heart of It All

When scientists tell us
Atoms are mostly
Made of nothing,
They are speaking
As priests charged
With a deep mystery:

How nothing holds
The universe together;
How nothing
Is the secret force
At the heart of it all.

In the old days, theologians
Asked: Is there an angel
Of nothing
Among the heavenly hosts?
The answer is No.

Nor does an angel
Of nothing dwell in hell.

Nothing is the only
Angel and cannot
Rise or fall.

All of us surround
The angel of nothing,
Whizzing our winged
Elliptical circuits of worship
Like electrons
Orbiting a nucleus.
With our restless fly-buzz
We create
The material world.

2. If They Bowed

The wisest among us
Always believed in
Nothing. When the lamp
Of faith went out,
They knew nothing
Remained. They knew
Nothing was there
Like a pillar
Of darkness,
Holding up the sky.
They knew nothing
Was necessary
To explain the way
Things were . . .

Some of them hid
Their belief
In nothing. Some
Even praised
The created world
And said they loved
Everything, but
Really nothing
Sat on their heart's
Throne and held sway.

If they bowed at all,
It was to nothing.
If they prayed,
They prayed to nothing.

Is dew on the grass
At sunrise nothing?
Is the vowel
Vibrating the open
Throat nothing?

Yes. Nothing
Surrounds us.
Nothing is inside us.
Nothing is the pure
Source where the soul
Kneels at dawn,
Where it drinks, then sings.

3. The Journey

Nothing guides you through the night
Woods. Nothing knows the way.
Nothing conducted all the old poets
When they were lost souls.
Nothing rose up in the form of a crow
Or a figure in a cone of light.
Nothing stood before them and said:
"I am here. You will not perish
Alone in the dark."
                  It's true
The lamp of faith has gone out.
It's true, the trees are a thicket
Of skeletal hands lifted to halt you.
It's true the strewn leaves hide
The path. But nothing is here
Beside you. Nothing will lead you.
You can depend on nothing.
To believe in nothing is the first step.

4. Its Function

Nothing stands between
The abyss and you.
Nothing keeps you
From falling off
The edge.
           Nothing
Is that important.

People think:
"There's always
Something
To chink up
The gaping cracks
In the ruined hut
Of self."

They're wrong.
There's nothing.

5. Letting In

I'm afraid I've let nothing
Into this poem.

It wasn't an easy decision
Because nothing
Is a difficult theme.

Of course, that's only
My opinion. Others
Disagree—many say:
Nothing is easy.
But I know better.
From my point of view,
Nothing is impossible.

That's why I've tried
To keep nothing
Out of this poem.

6. Some of Its Qualities

Nothing has a heart of gold.
Nothing waits up for you
Way past midnight.
Nothing thinks about you
All the time.
Nothing puts your interests
First. Nothing says:
"What would *he* want?"
"What would make *her*
Happy?"
        From the beginning
Nothing was on your side.
Nothing cares for you
More than your own
Mother did.
           Nothing loves you.

7. A Friend in Peril

"What's wrong?"
           "Nothing,"

She said.
    I saw right
Then she was in trouble.

Once nothing gets
Inside you, it's only
A matter of time
Before it's sliding
Along, smooth
As the little zeros
Of blood cells slipping
Through your veins.

Before you know it,
Nothing has become
Indispensable.
You can't imagine
Life without it.
        Soon,
Nothing is everything to you.

8. How I Became Involved

Quite early on, I discovered
Nothing mattered to me.
I felt nothing was near
My heart, but also
Integral to the universe.

I felt nothing explained
All the big questions:
Suffering, the sudden
Appearance of flowering
Plants, the origin
Of the cosmos. Nothing
Answered all enigmas
With a calm equanimity
I myself hoped to learn.

I modeled myself on nothing.
Not just the nothing I held
Close to my heart, but
A social nothing also: if
Nothing had been clothes,
I would have worn nothing.
If nothing was food, I
Would have eaten nothing.
If nothing was a way of talking,
I would have said nothing.

Nothing seemed to me
The answer to everything.
I remember clearly the moment
This came to me: it was dusk
And I was walking my dog
On our quiet street,
And the next thing I knew
I'd fallen to my knees,
Weeping for the joy of at last
Having understood nothing.

9. Some Facts About It

Nothing rides a black
Stallion big as the stars.
Nothing lives in a silver
City.
     Nothing makes a noise
Like wind in the pines.

10. My Own Conundrum

Many people believed I was committed
To nothing. They were wrong.
My allegiance was half-hearted
At best.
     I felt nothing could get
Along without me, and at the same time
I knew that nothing needed
My total loyalty.
     "Ambivalence,"
My doctor said.
     "No," I answered,
"A spiritual paradox that language
Aches to reveal.
     Nothing
Wishes to show itself to us
And nothing stands in its way."

11. A Committed Life

"What are you looking at?"
My mother asked.
         "Nothing,"
I answered.
         "I thought
So," and she turned away.

But I continued to study
Nothing. Noted its features,
Its calm demeanor; its smooth
Uninflected surfaces.
         Later,
In large books, I read
About nothing—theories
Of nothing, histories
Of nothing. Over the years,
Nothing revealed to me
Its heights and depths.

Almost without knowing it,
I had become an expert
On nothing. People sought
My opinion about it.
"Nothing is important,"
I told them.
         They were
Impressed. They lured me
To a great university;
They begged me to teach

All I knew about nothing.
It seemed only reasonable:
A final flowering of my life's
Passionate commitment to nothing.

12. Not Without Risks

Nothing has changed
For me.
          Gone are
Her smiles—
Transparent,
Terrifying.

Gone, the ways
In which
Nothing pleased me.

I think back to when
Nothing
Was everything
To me
And filled my world.

I was afraid
I would lose
Nothing if she changed.

My fears proved true.

13. That It Cares Deeply

So many people I loved
Are now a part of nothing.

Nothing took them in
Out of the cold
Where they stood,
Shivering and patient,
Hoping to again
Be part of something,
Which is,
Of course, impossible.

When you die, nothing
Has room for you.
Nothing makes a place
For you in its spacious
Domain.
       You dwell there,
And nothing cares for you.

*

Reading Dickinson

If you ask me, when God
Speaks
From the whirlwind,
The syllables He utters
Are guttural,
Crude, destructive.

I prefer Emily's music
That seems to issue
From a pool
Whose spiral motion
Is pulling her in and down.

Each poem is a whorled
Shell
I hold to my ear.

Roar of the Abyss?
Yes, but above it,
Her clear
And human voice,
Singing as she drowns.

Lines Standing in for Religious Conviction

Truth of it is: I was born
With an empty center.

When I find myself there,
It's often despair.
But now and then, it's Zen.

A leap of faith from a cliff?
I prefer hope
And bring my own rope.

A focused love is a doubled
Devotion—each shrine
I build deepens my mind.

Only when I yearn, do I learn.

And what helps me grow is holy.

Ode to Some Lyric Poets

> . . . certain poems in an uncertain world

1.

"Audacity of Bliss"—that's what
Emily Dickinson called it.

More than once I've felt it
And knew if I could
Turn it into words and share it,
I'd have a reason to live
And no matter
How badly
Life turned out, I could bear it.

I cherish that night she woke me
To hear her recite:

"Before and After—Vanished—
There is only—Now.

A Kiss—Appropriate
On its shining Brow."

Who only a year earlier,
Had appeared in another
Dream to announce:

"We are bound by words
And wonder to the world."

Then she scowled and smiled
At the same time,
And told me to write it down.

Who was I to disagree?

2. To Hart Crane

This huge bridge, cabled
Harp strung
Between two cities,
Heart stretched
Taut
Between two shores.

It's here you paused
Where others
Had stood
Who couldn't stand
The tension
And chose to leap.

You didn't—you chose to sing.

3.

Wilfred Owen's hunched
Over his shovel,
Muttering about
Corpse-stench, mustard gas.

And no matter how loud
I shout, he won't look up.

His ears are ruptured;
His brain, concussed
From gigantic artillery
Explosions.
    He's dug
Enough trenches
To fill the entire
Twentieth century,
Yet no line is deep enough
To save a single one of us.

4.

The mind "has cliffs" that are
"Sheer, no-man-fathomed,"
And Gerard Hopkins clung
To more than one.
    He knew
How vast and frightening
It can be inside

And never denied
His own brain was mostly
A landscape of chasms.

He descended, again
And again, clutching
Notebook and pen,
To the bottom
Of the deepest and darkest.

5.

Rimbaud, crashing
Through danger
And degradation—
Convinced
That on the other side
Resplendent wonder
Must abide.
                What courage
It took—his poems
Spitting off sparks
As they raced through the dark.

6.

When Karl Marx was beardless
And young, he wanted most
To be a poet.

He gave it
A shot, but it didn't click
And soon he switched
To other things for which
He became rightly famous,
For instance: the claim
That all labor ought to be sacred.

7.

> I believe in nothing but the holiness of the heart's
> affections and the truth of imagination.
>
> KEATS

I know it never
Happened:
       She's asleep
Now in the small room
They share.
       Keats
Is still awake
At his desk,
Feverishly
Trying to translate
Her body into words—
Those ripening breasts—
"Their soft fall and swell."

He pauses, puts hand
To chin and stares

Off into space—
A pose
He's perfected
For working on poems.

After a bit, he's restless
And stands up
To cross the room,
Lean down and,
With his lips,
Closely follow the original text.

8. The Lake Poets

Somber Wordsworth
Paced his closed-in garden
To the regular, iambic meters
He composed as he strolled;

How the wilder Coleridge,
When they went for walks,
Kept veering off the path
To scramble up steep
Slopes on hands and knees,
With urgent,
Spasmodic gestures—
Rhythms of his own poems.

9.

Wordsworth felt "the burden
Of this unintelligible world."

Luckily, we don't bear it alone—
The beloved's eager to help.

Didn't she carry it in poems, whole
Centuries before we were born?

Won't he be lugging it in songs,
Long after we're gone?

10. <u>For Hölderlin</u>

Who'd want to be
That plaster statue
Of the god Calm
Around whom
Chaos
Swirls and swarms?

Better to swim
Through harm
Than ride
So high above it
That we look
Down on suffering.

You must descend,
Love said,
You must embrace
What seeks to break you.

11.

"Chaos shimmering through a veil
Of order"—Novalis
Trying to define art,
But instead describing
The beloved, how her
Curves press against
Confining garments.

Always, Eros at the heart
Of it—the beloved
Bending over us,
His breath troubling
Our surface to get at our depths.

12.

Shakespeare noted: poets
Have a lot in common
With lunatics
And besotted lovers—
Except the poet's eyes
Are free to rove

"In a fine frenzy
Rolling," and so they
Take in both heaven
And earth (and add
"hell" as well)—
Take in all three realms,
And also
That wild one inside us.
Not to mention what's going on
In the beloved's head
And heart—that double
Mystery no one's ever
Solved.
How to untangle
It all and make it plain?

"Grab your pen," was
The Bard's advice.

His command?
"Write like crazy!
It's your only chance to stay sane."

13.

Clutching a bottle of wine,
Petrarch follows his shepherd
Guide. They're trudging up
The steep slopes of Mount
Ventoux.

What he's up
To is pretty much without
Precedent (at least
In the West):
                    Climbing
A mountain
Just for the fuck of it.

True, he's also one more
Trapped poet
Of the Middle Ages
Searching for some way out
That doesn't lead to God.

Now, he's reached the top
And suddenly gets it:
This huge vista his eyes
Are taking in—it
Mirrors the world inside.

Uncorking the bottle, he
Gazes south, frightened
But brave.
                    Biting
His lip hard, he tastes the sea.

14.

"The tears of things"—
Virgil's phrase;

As if every object
Is filled
With grief
And wants to weep.

When that dark mood
Weighs me down,
I feel the urge to cut
Each bright thread
That binds me to this world.

My body's a sad thing
I'd gladly leave behind—
Something I could
Step out of,
A long
Bandage I would unwind.

15.

"The whole country torn
By war. Only mountains
And rivers remain."
Du Fu's poem outlived
The strife it was born from.

History imposes its grim
Conditions: always,
The beloved is dying;
Always, rampant violence.

Always, the soul resists;
Someone somewhere
Is writing a poem,
And someone else waiting
(sometimes for centuries)
To read it—someone
Who needs it
So as not to yield to despair.

16. To Heraclitus

You taught the world's
Unstable—
Not even
Atoms are tame.

You showed
Change
Is the name
Of the game,
And even the game
Can change.

You never said strife
Was nice; only
That we need fire
As much as ice—
That energy

Must flow:
A structure
That's closed
Will only explode.

17.

Praxilla's single poem—
That made her
A fifth-century BC
One-hit wonder.
                    It briefly
Topped the charts:
Lament from that bleak
And cheerless Afterworld,
Which was the best
Greeks could imagine,
Even for their greatest heroes.

Those four lines—nothing
But a little list of things
Adonis missed most:

Stars and moon and sun
And the taste of ripe cucumbers.

Ode to Words

They cluster
At tongue-tip,
The points of pens.

Shaping them
Into word-ships—
That's my
Form of worship:

Riding the wild
River of this world.

*

The Bible says
Adam brought
Trouble
Into the world
With his small
Pink slab of muscle.

But if God didn't
Want it to happen,
Why did He
Give him a tongue?

*

"God so loved the word
He gave His only
Begotten world
That it might be
Redeemed."

I think the preacher
Used to say that
In my church
When I was a kid.

Then again, I could
Have gotten it wrong—
Back then
I wasn't really listening.

*

"And the word
Was made
Fresh"—

Each one
Baked daily.

It's the bread
By which I live.

*

Talk about miracles!
How I take empty air
Deep in my lungs,
Warming it there,
· Extracting from it
What my blood needs,

Then breathing it back
Out as sound
I've added meaning to.

*

Outside our bodies, things
Wait to be named,
To be saved.

And don't they deserve it?
So much hidden inside
Each one,
Such a longing
To become the beloved.

Meanwhile, the sounds
Crowd our mouths,
Press up against
Our lips
Which
Are such
A narrow exit
For a joy so desperate.

*

Vowels that rise
From our open throats . . .

Long "a" lounging, naked
In the leafy shade;
Then the low,
Lubricious moan of "o."

The high "e" of grief.

And "u"—who
Could ever forget you?

"I" could never.
"Y" would I even try?

*

The word "mockingbird"—
It's poised in my mouth

Same as the bird itself
Pauses on the dogwood branch.

When the bird flies away,
The word remains.

Look, now it's right here—
Singing on the page.

*

The word is exempt from
The world's flaws—

"Leaf" is complete,
Unscarred by insect
Or wind-tossed twig,

Yet it is an essence
That implicates the world
As a wound implies a body.

*

When I was young
I was always eager
To learn new words.
How many there were!

Now, I'm old and still
Learn new ones,
But forget more and more
Of those I once knew.

When I was young
I couldn't have imagined
The time would come
When I'd need so few.

*

I always supposed
It was words
I was after—
Those
Shining fish
The poem's net gets.

But who knows?
Maybe it was
The sea
Itself,
I was trying
To haul on deck.

Song of Lyric Geography

It consists of cliffs and plateaus—
The lyric life I chose.

In the worst phase, I know
Each desperate word
Is only a handhold
And there's a sheer fall below.

In the other, the pressure's
Suddenly gone,
And I stroll along
As calm phrases unfold;

Soon, I've become deluded—
My guard's down
And I'm convinced
It will *always* be like this:
A steady catalogue
Of my hard-earned bliss.

That's when it opens
Beneath my feet—recurrent abyss.

*

You sat alone in a room . . .

You sat alone in a room,
Listening to the harsh
Chorus
Of accusing voices.

Waiting for the worst
To pass, waiting for
The meanest to cease.

Hoping the beloved
Was somewhere
Among them;

Hoping—when
The malicious
Hubbub was over—
You'd hear one word of love.

There are questions . . .

There are questions
That must be asked,
But no one alive
Can answer,
And yours is one of them:

Where was the beloved
Then,
You want to know?

When, in the dark
Orchard, he hurt you.

When you curled up
In the tiniest ball
A child's body can be,
And still the blows fell?

The Undertoad

Something in words that's perverse,
That wants to be beyond
What we understand and control—
Something above or below.

"Watch out for the undertoad,"
Was what she heard her father
Shout above the waves—
That a word misheard could create
Such a creature
And feed her childhood fears.

Or how I mistyped "undertow"
As "undertown"
And found myself inhabiting
A city beneath the sea
Where everything moved slowly
And breathed chains of bubbles
That rose toward the upper world,
A tethering of pearls.

Trying hard just to listen . . .

Trying hard just to listen
And let the story enter,
Though I'm tempted
To turn away,

Or to use my own words
To put a wall between us.

Eager to reassure quickly,
As if compassion
Could save me
From my own fear.

How my ears burn
With the blush
Of what she confesses,

Or go cold and bloodless
As he tells of all he endured.

Aftermath Sonnet

Letting my tongue sleep,
And my heart go numb.

Sensing that speech
Too soon,
After such a wound,
Would only be
A different bleeding.

Even needing to leave
The page blank.
Long season
Of silence—
Trusting that under

Its bandage of snow,
The field of me is healing.

How often I've wished . . .

How often I've wished
It arrived by just
Sashaying in
Through my senses.

But for me, love
Couldn't enter
Until I was broken,
All the way to the center.

Right here, the blow fell—
A sledgehammer
Against a wall.
                And so,
A ragged door was made,
And the beloved came to dwell.

It's narrow . . .

It's narrow, and no room
For error—I zig

And zag through
The treacherous channel.

What fool said joy
Is less risky than grief?

My ship could wreck
On *either* shore.

Needing to navigate
By contradiction:

What I want to grip,
I need to release.

When despair says
"Let go," I must hold.

Aftermath Inventory

Shattered? Of course,
That matters.
            But
What comes next
Is all
I can hope to master.

Knowing, deep in my
Bones,
Not all hurt harms.

My wounds?
            If,
Somehow, I
Grow through them,
Aren't they also a boon?

My scars?
          Someday,
They might shine
Brighter than stars.

For Trisha

1.

They were your anchors—
Your parents.

Without them,
What can the boat do
But respond
To tides and currents?

In time, you'll hoist sail;
Rudder and keel intact.

You can navigate—
There are islands to find.

But when you get there—
There being anywhere—
What will hold you?
What will keep you from drifting?

2.

Grieving over something
You never even knew
You loved: that gloomy
House of your childhood

Where you were mostly
Miserable.
        Sold now,
And tomorrow a stranger
Will begin to live there.

Lighter and lighter as we grow
Older—stuff lost, or cast off.

3.

We're so near, but because of that,
Sometimes we need to shout.

We call it "clearing the air."
We're allowed to say mean things
As long as they're true, or seem so
In that moment.
                Also, they must be
Evenly matched—tit for tat.
And later, we have to take it all back.

We don't do this for fun. We do it
When one of us knows her heart's
In the right place, but no longer beating;

Or one of us notices his lungs are ok,
But he's no longer breathing.

4. Prayer/Plea

Come now, come soon, I summon you
Who, alone, can burst this husk
Of numb that I've become.

And bring your jumper cables,
Your battery juiced with blue fire—
I need its zap.
           I need you
And your voodoo lute. I need
One more of your rescues
Innumerable.
           Heed this, my howled plea
That's half-past last gasp:
                 I need you to
Horizon-happen, bringing the usual.

We were that joke . . .

We were that joke, a couple joined at the hip—
But such an oddity had its own appeal.
For us—the wounds kissed long before the lips.

Easy enough to get past the nasty quips:
How codependent we were; how unreal
And comically odd—a couple joined at the hip.

The risk of this: we're a single nerve from toe to tip—
When one is hurt, the other's bound to squeal.
The fate of those whose wounds kiss long before their lips.

The upside? Our lives are braided: two strips
Of soul-stuff wound together so we feel
That when our bodies couple at the hip

It's what the gods intended: a joy that rips
The heart out and serves it as a meal.
When your wounds have kissed long before your lips

Love will always be the bittersweet of whips—
The hurt will deepen long before it heals.
You learn such things when you're joined at the hip
And your wounds have kissed long before your lips.

Ode to the Country of Us

We made it up

Out of two pronouns:
"I" and "you."

We called it
The country of Us.

*

That first, exploratory meeting
Full of mutual suspicions—
How could they be
Overcome?
          In the beginning
It wasn't even certain
We spoke the same tongue.

At best, they were wildly
Divergent dialects.

A dictionary?
          Years
In the making.
           Key terms—
Still in dispute to this day.

*

From the outset,
It was hard for
Us
To see eye to eye.

For my part, I was
Distracted
By the rest of you.

*

If we were two ships
We could have passed
In the ocean and not
Known.
          If we were
Two birds we might
Have been flying
To opposite sides
Of the sky.
          But
We were two bodies
Who bumped
Into each other
And clung.
          Two
Bodies that collided,
Then steadied each other,
Then stayed.

*

Shortly after we met,
We held a contest
To design a flag.

I wanted a small
Yin-yang
Superimposed
On a labyrinth.

You favored a single
Rose,
Rising from a single vase.

We settled on something
Totally white—
It had nothing
To do with purity,
Nor with surrender.

Think of a blank page
On which experience
Will write lines
Indelible as those
That mark a face.

Think of a bed
With covers thrown back,
And the sheet beneath
Ready for the wars of love.

*

Our currency
Is touch.

A Kiss the single
Largest
Denomination.
Followed by
A Caress:
An open hand
Sliding down
An arm or
Squeezing a thigh.

Small change
The fingertips give.

*

No wonder it's unstable:
The national anthem
Never the same
For two consecutive days:

Whatever love song
The jukebox plays.

*

The stamps are also
Ridiculous.
Only two kinds:

If you're feeling
Friendly
You lather
Your lips thickly
With something
Red and smooch
The right-hand
Corner
Of the envelope.

If you're pissed
At the intended
Recipient,
You ink your thumb
And push down
Hard,
As if crushing an insect.

*

Who could possibly predict
The future of a country
As small as
Us?
    What are
Its prospects?

No army to speak of.
Some think
Its natural resources
All but exhausted.

Optimists insist
It will last our lifetime.

We can only hope.

*

Seeking the most
Accurate account?
You won't find it
In history books—

They get the facts,
But they don't
Get the mystery.

Poems and songs?
Saturated with lies;
Closest
You'll come to the truth.

*

Nostalgia: a national
Pastime—
Whole days spent
Conjuring up
A lost
Golden moment,

Or lavishing
A nacreous beauty
Around a grit of fact.

*

Thrive though it might, its days
Are necessarily numbered.

You don't need to see
A crack in the wall,
To know mortality calls.

Who'll be the one to leave?
Who, the one to grieve?

*

Briefest of nations—
Blip
On history's screen.

Leaving not even
A trace
Of its existence.

To the world
It was
Less than nothing.

To us: it was all.

*

Sitting at a dinner table . . .

Sitting at a dinner table
With seven old people,
The youngest among us
In her mid-sixties.
Eating and drinking
And talking along;
The men dominant
And pompous
And name-dropping
As each in turn
Mounts his hobbyhorse
And gives a little lecture
(myself included).

And the topic of written
Words comes up
And one of the women
Wisely observes
That the tablets of Moses
Gave the Jews of Genesis
A way to behave—
Got them back on a path
To basic decency
If not to a promised land.

And I respect that: writing
Out a few, clear-cut
Prohibitions wasn't

A bad idea;
And when you toss in
A little Sumerian
Eye-for-an-eye
And tooth-for-a-tooth,
You've got a rough version
Of justice, as well as some
Good rules.
   And so,
We Western humans began
Our stumble through history,
Our endless and uncertain
Struggle against the worst
In us and the worst
Among us—those
Who delight in power
And, in turn, recruit
Those who take
Pleasure in harming others.

By now, the wine's not
Working anymore
And I'm silently reflecting
On how I've lived through
The end of one century
Into the next, and still
It's a dark and violent world.

The Ferris Wheel at the World's Fair

The wheel swoops you up, swoops you down again.
The giddiest ride in the world, they swear.
When you're high, you're high, but where does it end?

You take your seat and then your seat ascends
And far below you: bright lights of the fair.
The wheel swoops you up, swoops you down again.

When you're high, stars and neon blur and blend
But don't get off, unless you walk on air.
When you're high, you're high, but it will end.

They look so small down there, your former friends.
Like ants or insects. Who could really care?
But the wheel that swoops up, swoops down again,

And when it does, when the big wheel descends,
You'll step off dizzy. You'll want someone there
When all your highest highs begin to end.

Fortune has a zero for a heart—defend
Against Her, whose wheel is noose and snare.
It swoops you up to swoop you down again.
It takes you high, but all highs have their end.

Dark Proverbs for Dark Times

> In the dark times
> Will there also be singing?
> Yes, there will also be singing.
> About the dark times.
> BERTOLT BRECHT

The smart hide their claws
In their paws,
Then add fur for allure.

Combining smiles and wiles
And calling it "style."

*

Dark *and* deep?

A dangerous creep.

*

A corporation is a person
And has certain rights.

A crow is a cow
And gives milk at night.

*

A sword may
Have a point,

But a needle
Is sharper
And cleaner.

Less mess;
Less evidence.

*

Does a man with a bow
Deserve a bow?

Only if he also has arrows.

*

Deep pools lure fools.
Shallows attract rascals.

*

Blood and tears
Grease history's gears.

*

Minds are deeper
Than mines.

And twice as dark.

*

Those with towers favor power.

*

A good journey calls
For survive
As well as arrive.

Stay alert: sharks
Don't bark;
Nor do bears share.

When demons
Appear, be aware,
But don't stare.

*

Verifiable perils:

Who lives must lie.
Too many, and you die.

*

Remember: every fist
Began as an open hand.

Even a bridge is a ledge
If you stray to its edge.

*

All atrocities
Breed
Reciprocity:

Every murder
Leads to further.

*

Those who praise rage
Should be made

To visit more graves.

Skulls annul.
All knives should be dull.

*

None have done wrong
Who still have a tongue.

Even Cain can explain.

I Don't Really Care, Do You?

I don't really breathe,
Do you?
             I don't really
Think. Do you?
                    I don't
Actually wake up
In the morning
And open my eyes. Do you?

Do you really?
                    How interesting.
Perhaps you've seen
What's happening.
I really don't care. Do you?

Maybe you could do
Something about it—
Turn the stars inside out,
Raise the sea level
Another inch next week
(in this real-time repeat,
God's flood is too slow,
as if He was trying to give us
time to think).
                    Or why not
Raise the dead?
                    That hasn't
Been done for a while.

(I don't really care. Do you?)
You could begin with the dead
Who bled in the street,
And then move on to those
Whose deaths were less obvious,
Whose lives leaked out
Invisibly while they were asleep.

So many of them—
It would be hard work:
Dead in the brain, dead in the heart.

It's just an idea—somewhere to start.

Charlottesville Elegy

There's a single eye that hovers
Above this city, hovers
By day and by night.

You might assume
It's the sun or the moon,
But I've lived here
Forty years
And never seen it before.

It isn't the bitter eye
Of racism, which haunts
Alleys and grocery aisles;
Nor the icy eye of privilege—
I've seen that many times,
Shining above the university
Or gazing down
On Farmington's lawns,
Groomed
Smoother than golf greens.

It's not the Internet's eye,
That can't sleep
For the fever dreams
It breeds.
   Not the secret eye
Of the pine's cut stump;

Nor the eye of the poor
That has seen it all.

It's not the black eye
Of notoriety,
Nor the blue one of denial.

It's not the State's blank eye,
Made of papier-mâché,
Nor the eye of the police
That was looking the other way.

It's not the eye of violence
That would strike
Lightning if it could;
Nor the eye of love
That sees, but doesn't judge.

Neither is it Jefferson's eye,
Inert in bronze repose;
Nor that of Sally Hemings,
Startled even in eternity.
(It's certainly not
God's eye—
that turned away eons ago.)

It's not the eye of witness,
That winced;
Nor the eye of grief
That wept briefly,

Then resumed its journey
Through
This ruthless world.

Undeceived, unassuageable eye;
Remorseless eye—
It's come to remind our city
Of a proverb
Older than the Pyramids:

If you've closed one eye to evil,
You'd better not blink.

Hector Bidding Wife and Child
a Last Good-bye

Soon enough, the gods will keep their nasty
Promise and Achilles' spear will pierce
His chest. But now, for all its scars
And imperfections, his body is still whole
Beneath his wife's caress.
                  It rests
On the floor—his helmet plumed
With a horsehair crest that, in battle,
Shakes wildly and makes him appear
Taller and more fierce than he really is.

Only a moment ago, as he took it off,
It scared his young son,
Who cried in terror
And ran from the room, never to see him again.

Downtown Tour

Here's our park: civic
Cathedral of trees,
Green floor where
Pagan congregations
Sprawl.
      Tucked
In a corner (shabby
chapel dedicated
to the god of war):
A bronze colonel
On horseback, pointing
East with his sword
(pity those who
followed him—
they ended up in the sea).

Best, the old Greeks
Said, never
To be born at all.
I'd say: Next best
Is to lie low
With someone
You love
On a spot like this:

A raft of grass
Smaller
Than the smallest

Battlefield,
Bigger than
The biggest mattress.

Lyric Revises the World

According to some, an army
Marching or cavalry charging,
Or a raiding fleet under sail,
Is the loveliest sight
On this black earth, but *I* say:
Whatever one loves most is beautiful . . .

SAPPHO (FROM FRAGMENT 16)

Sappho, you started it all off
With your pithy remark:
"Whatever one loves most
is beautiful."
                        Until you
Spoke up, who knew
The personal
And passionate heart
Was what created value?

Who knew we *each*
Had power
To say what mattered?

All around you, the guys
Jabbered on and on
About how awesome
Marching armies are,
How their hearts fluttered
When the cavalry charged.

But you had the nerve
To disagree
And insist on details
Both tender and specific—
What William Blake
Would later
Call the "minute particulars."

Not for you, those things
Hugely violent
That shook the earth
And only existed to hurt,
But rather what was intimate,
Personal, scaled to the human:

Your daughter Kleis, "golden
as a flower,"
Or Anactoria, your lover—
The way her hips
Moved when she walked, her smile.

Ode to These Socks

Here I am sitting on the porch
Of my cottage
Wearing a pair
Of bright new socks
That you might think
You recognize
From Pablo Neruda's ode,
But these are a pair
I bought myself
So my feet could be
Warm on a cool
May morning like this.

The socks aren't cool at all,
But "hot," with swirling
Bands of red and blue
Like a psychedelic
Barber pole except
There is no white
And so no irony about
The American flag,
Although
They were probably
Knitted by some
Poor son of a bitch
On a huge machine in China—
A former peasant
Who now works

A fifteen-hour shift
And sleeps in a small room
In the factory dormitory
With ten others who don't
Even speak his dialect—
And all for pennies a day
And a thousand miles
From his mountain home,
While I sit here in Virginia
And pull on these bright socks
Against the late May chill.

Nor is my ode about
Imperialist guilt
Or even its dark twin—
The global economy—
Because after all, they
Will win soon, and someday
His descendants
Will feel they rule
This foolish and suffering world.

So I'm guessing the moral
Of my ode has more to do
With the mystery
Of it all:
          How being alive
Is probably the best
That most of us
Can accomplish,
Though gratitude

For what we've received
Is the least we can feel,
Not to mention compassion
For those
Who suffer endlessly,
And may never get a glimpse
Or wink of joy.
                    And my luck
Seems double luck
Because it's so gratuitous,
Because I never did a thing
To earn it, and yet
It's come to me, as has
This morning
With its early light slanting
Through the maple trees
Alive with birdcalls
And me looking out
On the innocent day
With the eyes I was given for free.

Coleridge and Me

Old now, nearer my own last
Poem, I think of Coleridge:
How much he left unfinished.

There he was: a young man
Stoned on opium, glimpsing
That imaginary garden
For the first time . . .
                    Even then,
He was beginning to suffer
Agonies of procrastination
That would shadow all his days.

He believed in a Christian heaven.
I don't. I prefer Paradise,
Which comes from a Persian word
For "walled garden"—
A green and fountained place
In a world that's mostly bleak
(and which works for me
as one good definition of poetry).

I hope Coleridge is there, safe
From the hell of this world
Or any other.
            And I hope
Somehow it's been completed
And he lives inside it:

That stately pleasure dome
He and Kubla Khan
Began, so many years ago.

Emily Dickinson Test-Drives
the First Home Sewing Machine

Rain thrums a tattoo
On her window, the same
Excruciating pattern
Her needle dots into fabric.

Emily's bent over the Singer,
Pumping the treadle
For all she's worth
And look what emerges:
A white dress stitched
With black, zigzag
Lightning seams of language
And fitful bits of rhyme
On cloth thin as tissue,
Thin as skin.
            She's
Making another bridal
Shroud, another festive
Gown to be packed away
In the attic, that grave
That hovers above us.

Road-dust on her window
(stuff someone's journeying
horse and buggy churned up)
Mingles now with the rain
To form soft rivulets.

It's thus the dust dissolves
And when the sun comes again,
Her mystery's intact, her pane
Shines bright and blinding
To all our prying eyes.

Into a thousand pieces?

Into a thousand pieces?
Must this rending
Really precede mending?

Scattered everywhere?
Some, lost in the dark,
As if never
To be found again?

Maybe life's trying
To tell me
My heart
Was too small.

Now I start to regather,
And when I'm done
Maybe it will be larger—

A thousand and one.

Some phrases move . . .

Some phrases move
Slow as a worm,
Chewing
A tunnel
Through dirt.
Others, swift as a bird.

Always, it's the beloved
They're seeking.

She could be hiding
Above;
He could be
Buried below.

Sorrow-songs, trying
Their best
To digest
The thick dark.

Songs of joy—
Whizzing past
So fast, they're
Gone before we notice.

Ode to Left-Handedness

I sat at my kindergarten desk,
Surrounded by others,
Either cheerful
Or bored, who were
Cutting
The requisite circles
With ease,
Or slicing down
Straight, penciled lines
As the teacher directed.

I did my dutiful best,
But the scissors
Hurt my fingers
In a minor,
Distracting way,
And I was too young
To realize the handle
Was biased
For a right-hand child,
So all I could do
Was cut in clumsy zigzags
And feel like a fool.

Staring hard at the blades,
I tried to *will* them
To obey,
Who couldn't conceive

I was being freed
That day
By those little silver wings
Of a bird
Intent on the erratic,
Authentic pattern
Of its own flight
Through a sky of colored paper.

Certain poems offer me . . .

Certain poems offer me escape—
They're floating islands
Anchored only
By a cloud-rope of words
I can climb.
          Some
Are the opposite:
Insisting on
Embodiment—
As if they were tattooed
On the beloved's thigh.

Still others are short
And sharp—arrows
Aimed at the heart,
As if the purpose
Of beauty
Was to hurt me more alive.

For weeks now . . .

For weeks now, I've been
Lost in the maze
Of spring's profusions;
Lazily wandering
Around, neglecting
So much,
Ignoring my garden.

Heeding instead
The willow's green
Singing—
Imagining it was
The beloved.

Listening to the frogs'
Chorus and
Thinking so, also.

And now a pair
Of wrens
Has given me
A comeuppance:

They've built their nest
In my weeding basket
That hangs
From a hook in the open shed—

Three round, pale eggs!

Still Life

For Trisha

The purpose, of course, is to hold life still,
To turn the fleeting shadow into shade,
Though such a purpose is against life's will.

Lace and quilts and flowers like a bird's quills—
Praising what you've rescued from time's blade
Is the purpose, of course. But to hold life still

Can itself raise strange questions: Does it kill
Them differently to have their deaths delayed?
It's clear our purpose is against life's will:

Life prefers the running water to the still;
In *its* world, tulips only bloom to fade.
Our purpose, though, is to hold life still

So the harried gazer can gaze her fill
At this rich jumble purposefully arrayed,
Though such a purpose is against life's will.

What it means is this: vital moments that spill
Into that quiet space a painting's made.
The purpose, of course, is to hold life still
Though such a purpose is against life's will.

For My Daughters

Fearing for them, I
Clustered them together,
Then cut them off
From others—
Cloistered them
As if they were nuns.

As if they could only
Stand a little suffering
And needed shielding.

Maybe the opposite's
True—they long to be
Tested.
     Maybe
Something inside them
Prowls the space I made,
Eager to leap forth
When hurt at last
Smashes open their cage.

For My Mother

Driving at night over the back
Roads, you used
To sing old songs.

My favorite was
"Down in the Valley"—
Melancholy tune
Whose refrain went:
"Angels in heaven
Know I love you."

You were soon
To die and me
Still a child, sitting so
Close beside you,
Yet mishearing
That line as if it
Paused in the middle
While the singer
Considered
A celestial offer
And then declined:

As if it meant
"Angels in heaven?
No, I love you."

Such a choice
Impressed me,
And even then made sense.

The last love poem I will ever write . . .

Will contain an invention for turning ants' tears
Into hummingbird wings. It will hold every
Elegy the night sky ever wrote for the moon.
It will reveal the answer to the question "Yes."

It will feature a rosebush that grew naturally
Into the shape of a woman, a man, and a dog.
It will contain all our sorrow and some of our joy.

It will exhibit glass slippers worn by the last queen of mice
And also the invisible cathedral built on the spot where we met.
It will display a tree whose leaves change color
With the weather, turning bright blue at forty degrees.

It will contain a replica of the ice ship that sails
Through dreams, searching for survivors.
It will contain all our joy and most of our sorrow.

Young, I took it all so . . .

Young, I took it all so
Personally
When things vanished.

There's a word for that:
Inconsolable.

You'd think, as I
Grew older,
I'd have adjusted
To the simple fact
That everything's
Borne away
On a ceaseless flood.

But then, I'd never have
Become
A lyric poet—

Someone with a grudge
Against the world,

Against the world he loves.

Secret Constellation

From start to finish
It must have been
There.
      How else
Could I have begun
As a kid
Bent
Over a desk,
Trying to guess
What shape
My pencil
Would make
When at last
It connected up
That cloud
Of numbered dots,

And ended up
Here:
An old man,
Happily
Staring into
An inner dark
Strewn
With words
Like random stars?

Some luminous
Pattern
Must have
Ruled my days.
From start
To finish,
It must have been there.

Inscription

All this winter afternoon spent
Reading about ancient
Greek lyric and the invention
Of the simple alphabet—
How those small marks
On papyrus changed
Everything; persuaded
Lyric poets they could
Become immortal.
                        "Someone
Will remember us,"
Wrote Sappho, naming
Herself and those she loved
In poems that are only
Fragments now,
And a single one that's whole:
A prayer to Aphrodite.

An old man with a full
Bladder, I pause
To step out back
Where yesterday's flurries
Have made the lawn
Into a blank page
In a small corner of which
I piss out the hot stream
Of my own being,
Grateful to be part of that

Holy and hopeless story
By which poets send past death
Their praise of life
And write
Their names on the vanishing page.

It's time . . .

It's time to turn the TV off
And listen.
                    That noise?
What is it?
Maybe it's only crickets.

Maybe it's distant music.
Maybe people
Are dancing somewhere
Not far from here,
The beloved among them.

Out into the street—
We need to investigate,
To find out what's there.

Even if it's only crickets.

Acknowledgments

Some of these poems, some in earlier or different forms, have appeared in the following magazines:

American Poetry Review: "Ode to Some Lyric Poets,"
    "Lines Standing in for Religious Conviction," "Dark
    Song," "And So," "Ode to Words."
Mississippi Review: "Dark Proverbs for Dark Times"
    appeared originally as "Three Dark Proverb Sonnets"
    and was subsequently chosen by Natasha Trethewey to
    appear in *Best American Poetry 2017* (Scribner's).
Narrative: "Ode to Nothing," "The Ferris Wheel at the
    World's Fair," "Dark Proverbs for Dark Times," "I
    Don't Really Care, Do You?," "Charlottesville Elegy,"
    "Hector Bidding Wife and Child a Last Good-bye,"
    "Downtown Tour," "Lyric Revises the World," "Ode to
    These Socks."
Plume: "Sitting at a dinner table . . . ," "Song of What
    Happens," "The Ferris Wheel at the World's Fair."
Smartish Pace: "For Trisha," "Ode to the Country of Us,"
    "It's time . . ."
Well Review (Ireland): "How often I've wished . . ." and
    "Song of Aftermath."

My gratitude to the editors for their hospitality.